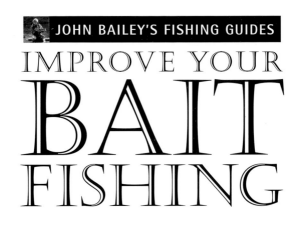

JOHN BAILEY'S FISHING GUIDES

IMPROVE YOUR

BAIT

FISHING

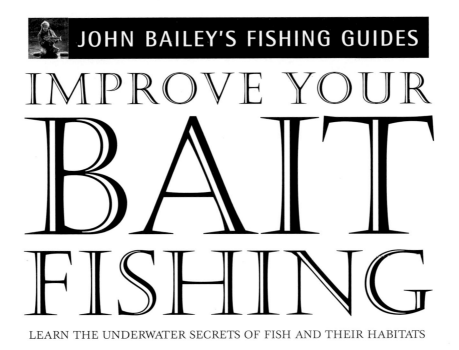

JOHN BAILEY'S FISHING GUIDES

IMPROVE YOUR BAIT FISHING

LEARN THE UNDERWATER SECRETS OF FISH AND THEIR HABITATS

First published in 2003 by
New Holland Publishers (UK) Ltd

London • Cape Town • Sydney • Auckland

www.newhollandpublishers.com

10 9 8 7 6 5 4 3 2 1

Garfield House, 86–88 Edgware Road, London W2 2EA

80 McKenzie Street, Cape Town 8001, South Africa

14 Aquatic Drive, Frenchs Forest, NSW 2086, Australia

218 Lake Road, Northcote, Auckland, New Zealand

ISBN 1 84330 354 X

Edited and designed by Design Revolution Limited,
Queen's Park Villa, 30 West Drive, Brighton BN2 2GE
Project Editor: Ian Whitelaw
Designer: Lindsey Johns
Editor: Julie Whitaker
Illustrations by Rob Olsen

Index by Indexing Specialists,
202 Church Road, Hove BN3 2DJ

Publishing Manager: Jo Hemmings
Senior Editor: Kate Michell
Assistant Editor: Anne Konopelski
Production Controller: Lucy Hulme

Reproduction by Pica Digital (Pte) Ltd, Singapore
Printed and bound in Singapore by Craft Print
(Pte) Ltd

Contents

INTRODUCTION

I have been catching fish on bait since 1956, and I've been watching with fascination the ways in which fish react and respond to bait since about 1958. I've been using tanks to study how fish behave since 1959 on and off – more frequently on, it has to be said. Over the last five years I have extended these observations by swimming with fish under water. I firmly believe that the close study of fish is central to any angler's understanding of his quarry, and that understanding is a vital part of catching. This book contains over 180 photographs that I believe convey core messages for the angler, but there are certain basic facts about fish and their environment that photographs cannot demonstrate, so please take on board the following observations.

▲ **A Good Sport** Goodness knows I've taxed the patience of my fishing fellows. All poor Chris wants to do is catch a barbel, when suddenly I invade, managing to get his line round my leg in the process!

SENSE AND SENSITIVITY

I know that fish are supposed to have a brain the size of a pea, a pinhead or whatever, and that scientists have proved they have memory spans of seconds. Well, speaking empirically, I cannot believe this at all. From what I've learned as an angler and seen as a diver, fish can remember unpleasant experiences for a very long time. It may take three or four sharp knocks for the message to sink home – and some fish undoubtedly learn more quickly than others – but once it has, fish can take a very long time to become 'uneducated' again. In short, unless conditions are very much on his side, the average angler faced with a swim full of wised-up barbel, for instance, will be very lucky to catch more than a tiny percentage of them. The message? Do not underestimate your quarry; afford them respect. If you're not catching, think hard about the reasons; change your approach and/or your bait. Keep working at it.

Water is a great conductor of sound, and fish are exceedingly receptive to any noise they are unused to or frightened by. The crunch of a boot on a gravel bank can spook a whole shoal of barbel for an hour or more. The sound of a bomb

▲ **IN ITS ELEMENT** Fighting a fish from the bankside is exhilarating enough, but wait until you see the action from below – only then can you fully appreciate the power and grace of a good fish.

or feeder hitting the water is thunderous and can send a whole shoal of chub fleeing in an instant. I've seen remote-water carp alarmed by a car door slamming nearly half a mile away. Keep bankside noise to a minimum and always think about how you can introduce bait and tackle as silently as you can.

The question of fish's eyesight I've not even begun to work out. I'm not going to dabble in scientific theory here – you can get that from any textbook. I'll simply stick to my own observations. There are times when fish can seem as blind as bats… watching roach groping for a lump of flake the size of a walnut, for example. However, the vast majority of the time, most fish species seem almost uncannily capable of seeing line, leads, floats and anything else we throw at them. Wised-up fish will make quite evident moves to sidestep all these things. All of which leaves me in absolutely no doubt about why we fish well in coloured water – the fish are simply less able to see the fine detail that they can in clear conditions. The message here is to make every aspect of your tackle as inconspicuous as possible – over-obvious line, shot, leger weights, even a glinting hook, can deter a fish from coming close to your bait.

THE LIVING WATER

Water is a strange element, constantly able to amaze. For example, I'm always fascinated by the power of underwater currents in stillwaters and by the very noticeable temperature changes here and there around a lake... and I'm not talking about deep diving down to the thermocline. The sinuous energy and sheer power of a river can be mind-boggling. Believe me, rivers don't just bulldoze doggedly to the sea – they can twist and turn in a staggering variety of ways. Therefore, look at water with new eyes; try to regard it in three dimensions – almost as a living creature. Remember that the river is the whole universe to the fish that inhabit it, and it influences them entirely.

THE CONSIDERATION THEY DESERVE

It seems to me that fish have very ordered lives that they lead in a well laid out way. They are very good at knowing exactly which part of their water will provide them with the best conditions for feeding, resting, or whatever their bodies tell them is necessary. Big shoal fish I find particularly interesting. Many of them form allegiances for one reason or another and will appear inseparable over weeks, months, and perhaps even years. They have a good deal in common with humans. It's only crises that force them out of their preferred routines, such as flood, drought, pollution, predatory attacks – and angling. It's worth remembering, therefore, that every time we catch or hook a fish we make a noticeable impact on both it and its fellows. Let us fish, by all means, because by fishing we are

▼ **A TRUE FRIEND** From the first page, I must acknowledge my debt to Johnny Jensen, Danish photographer, writer, angler, diver and, above all, travelling partner, inspiration and great friend.

▲ **SWIMMING WITH THE ENEMY** The underwater world is full of surprises – such as this stickleback that I watched living with a group of predatory chub!

guarding the aquatic environment, but do let us minimize the disruption we cause. Outside matches, let's do without keep nets. If bank space allows, catch one or two fish and then move on before the life of the shoal is disrupted.

For me, diving has re-emphasized how gloriously beautiful fish are, and it has taught me that they are even more so in their environment. I've also witnessed how long a wound inflicted by a pike – or by a bad unhooking technique – can take to heal. So let's treat fish with all the respect we can muster. Let's handle our fish as gently and as little as we can. As the saying goes, they're certainly worth it.

FOR THE TECHNICAL

I won't go into the intricacies of diving equipment here: a standard dry suit and all the equipment that goes with it is all that is needed. Sometimes extra-heavy weights are vital to pin you down to the bottom. Less important are flippers: I've done very little swimming over the last three or four years – mainly just sitting waiting on the bottom!

In terms of camera equipment, I have used Nikon F90Xs with a range of Nikon lenses; the most useful have been 24 and 28mm. I have generally used the Nikon speed light SB-28 when extra light has been needed. For a lot of the work I have made use of a Subal metal unit; this is very solid and trustworthy. For lighter, more mobile work I have used a Ewa-marine plastic bag. This may sound a bit flimsy, but it has only let me down once! Believe me, a flood is what every underwater photographer fears more than anything. Films have been uniformly Fuji. Provia 100 has been preferred, but at times of low light I've moved to 200 or 400 ASA speeds.

I hope that some of my underwater observations will throw light on the challenges that we, as anglers, meet on the bankside. Good luck.

John Bailey, Salthouse, Norfolk

HOW BARBEL BEHAVE

Like all members of the carp family, barbel lead generally ordered lives, but they also reveal fascinating behavioural abnormalities, both as individuals and as shoals, in the face of crises or problematic situations.

The more I watch barbel from below the water-line, the more I realize that there is a very apparent sifting process going on as they garner all the information they can from their environment. Many hours of barbel watching suggest they are neither blinkered nor stupid, but, indeed, are very aware of all the possibilities around them. They also have the ability to take fast, decisive action based on their observations.

For the angler, perfect barbel-watching water will be clear and relatively shallow, with good vantage points from islands or high banks. Good light is needed, and the barbel behave more naturally when the river is quiet.

▲ SEARCHING Barbel are quite happy to come into shallow water, where they find rich pickings under rocks and stones. Caddis are top of the list, but they also seek out snails, beetles, shrimps and small fish.

Traditional Feeding Behaviour

Barbel like to feed in a leisurely fashion, generally in groups – companionship, I am convinced, is very important to the species, and they actually choose to touch when they can. They often concentrate on patches of open gravel and stones, where they look for all manner of insect life. Angling pressure tends to restrict daylight feeding, and during daylight hours they don't tend to move too far from the comfort zone of snags and overhangs. Barbel of a reasonable weight will happily nudge rocks the size of a house brick out of the way to get at the caddis hiding beneath. The fish I witnessed in one Bohemian river had very noticeable cuts and scabs on their snouts from feeding amongst the endless rough boulders.

When feeding fish chance on a bed of bait, such as assorted pellets, their feeding becomes much more concentrated and the barbel group closer together. Any small fish – especially minnows – that have been pecking at the pellets quickly move out of the way, dropping downstream to feed in the drifting silt.

Look for clouded water, the tips of fins in the shallows and, especially the coral pink of the pectorals. On a sunny day, look for a shadow rather than the fish itself. Take your time, and observe an area of water closely before moving on. Often, the shapes of fish take a while to emerge, but once you have a suspicion, focus intently on the prime spot. Polaroid glasses and binoculars also help the detection process. Above all, look out for 'flashing' barbel (see pages 14–15).

▶ **FEEDING HARD** This barbel was photographed at a depth of five feet in a moderately clear river at 9am on a September morning. It is feeding hard, in the company of five other fish, turning over small stones and dislodging quantities of silt that form obvious clouds behind it.

◀ **FEEDING CONFIDENTLY** It is midday in flaming June in Andalucia, central Spain, and this barbel is happy to come into very open water, less than two feet deep, in full light. This may be because there is virtually no angling pressure here. This fish is doing what barbel like doing most – feeding over, under and around stones for caddis grubs, their preferred food item.

◀ **FAVOURITE FOOD** You can see why barbel turn rocks over. This one reveals a wealth of caddis larva cases, some empty and abandoned, but several still inhabited and ready to eat. There are times of the year when these food items make up the bulk of the barbel's diet.

◀ **ALERT AND SUSPICIOUS** The leading barbel has come up against the angler's lead, hook length and bait. The barbel is immediately alert and suspicious. There is no mistaking the way it arches its back and flares its fins – look at that gash of white along the root of the dorsal fin. In an instant, the fish stops feeding, backs off and drops ten yards downstream.

▶ GROUP FEEDING Again in Andalucia, we see how barbel like to feed. These fish are close to the bank in three feet of clear water, and though they are feeding hard in the area directly in front of them, they are still aware of larger food items further away. The rear fish has just eaten a crayfish that left the shelter of a stone and appeared in open water about four feet to the left of the barbel, which was on it in an instant. Examples like this increase my faith in big-impact baits, such as lobworms, dead fish or anything large and out of the ordinary.

▶ TEAM PLAYER I have already stressed that the barbel is normally a team player and operates best in groups – from two fish to several hundred. I have observed shoal members sticking together for many years; in the right circumstances they will probably live out their lives together, and there are obvious reasons for this. For one thing, a group of fish can detect potential danger more easily than a lone fish, but there are other mutual benefits. Feeding strategy is certainly one of them, and this may be one of principal explanations for barbel 'flashing' (see pages 14–15).

▶ HUDDLING TOGETHER Once again you can see the barbel very close together, bodies touching, fins draping each other, typical of a group that is distressed. Few anglers realize that a clumsy approach to any given swim can immediately result in this huddling action. Heavy footfalls on gravel, the banging in of a rod rest or even the noisy introduction of cannonballs of groundbait can thoroughly alarm a barbel grouping.

How and Why Barbel 'Flash'

There cannot be a single barbel angler who hasn't watched that thrilling stab of silver in the water, the sign of a barbel 'flashing' – turning onto its flank and letting the light illuminate it for a give-away second. But what is in the mind of a flashing barbel as it declares its presence in this way?

Feeding strategy appears to be one of the explanations for some flashing patterns, but there are numerous times that barbel flash when they are apparently not at all interested in feeding. There are no definite answers to why barbel flash when they are not feeding, but suggested reasons include communication, hygiene and territorial instinct.

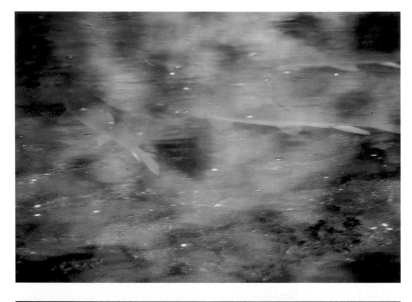

◀ **TELL-TALE SIGNS** These Spanish barbel exhibit dramatically the signs the observant barbel fisher should be looking out for. Who could miss the glint of these yellow stomachs as the fish twist and turn to get at the grains of scattered corn? Look out, too, for the coral-shaded pectoral fins of the barbel – another definite give-away.

◀ **DIVING FOR FOOD** It is late summer, and this is the lead fish of a shoal. In six feet of water, it repeatedly rises off the bottom, steadies itself in the current and then nosedives, wriggling – and flashing – along the river-bed for three or four feet before righting itself and continuing normally. This action creates a silt channel close to the bed, and the followers hurry into it to feed on insects that have been disturbed.

▶ **Communicating?** In the course of a morning, this seven-pound male barbel has moved rapidly around one area some dozen times, flashing fifteen to twenty times on each circuit. It is now late May, just a few weeks before spawning, so is this the issue? Is it somehow marking its territory? Or is this simply a fishy example of joie de vivre? For certain, this is a flashing barbel that is not feeding.

▶ **Parasites** It is late April, and the barbel are on the move after the lengthy winter period of inaction. This individual is grinding its body on stones. It's flashing, but it's not feeding and is alone. A closer inspection reveals that its flanks and fins are infected with *Argulus* fish lice, which may have been picked up during the winter when it barely moved from the bottom of the pool. So, is it now scraping itself free of its parasitic tormentors?

▶ *Argulus* **Scars** Fish lice typically attach themselves at the base of the tail stock or close to the fins. When they drop off, the lice leave red, irritated sores, such as these behind the pectoral fin of a barbel from the River Wye in Herefordshire.

Unexpected Feeding Behaviour

Barbel will always amaze and excite us with the diversity of their behaviour. Part of their charm is that they are largely unknowable. Just when you think you understand them, they do something so bewildering that you feel you're back at square one, and just as amazed as you ever were.

Unthreatened, stable shoals, which can number over a hundred fish but are sadly becoming more and more rare, will feed at all hours of day and night, and both at the surface and down at the bottom. Such shoals are comfortable with their surroundings and will glean food from all locations rather than concentrating in corners and shadows, as angler-threatened barbel tend to do. The barbel will also use the strength of their size and their apparent companionship to exploit a food source – I have seen two, and even three, barbel physically join forces to co-operate in pushing over a particularly heavy stone to get at the food beneath. However, barbel are not alone in this technique, other fish species, such as sea lamprey, will also collaborate to hunt out well-hidden food.

Barbel can be phenomenally adaptable – I have even seen them feeding upside down in fast water so that they can hoover insects from the roof of an overhang. They are also tactical hunters, and barbel looking for a large feed are happy to wait until enough fry gather and then herd them to the surface, picking them off in the top few inches of the water. Sometimes, the force of their upward surge can carry them right out of the water, and they fall back with a characteristic splash.

▲ **FALLEN TREES** It is July, and a group of twenty or so barbel have taken to living amongst the water-logged branches of a fallen tree. Hovering side by side, they are scraping all manner of edible material from the branches. They are also preying on the shoals of minnows and fry that seek shelter here.

▲ **OPEN-WATER FEEDING** I have never felt more privileged in my fishing life than when watching this shoal of barbel on the River Wye – something I did repeatedly for over three years, until the shoal was disturbed by angling pressure. Close on two hundred barbel lived in this swim, sometimes in two or three groups, sometimes joining together in one huge group. They were happy to spend the majority of the daylight hours drifting up and down on the surface, rarely going to the bottom except to feed early or late in the day. It was a very stable shoal, with individual fish recognizable within it.

▶ **ALL-DAY FEEDING** The fish of the Wye shoal were happy to feed at any time of the day. Any emerging fly would be taken, and they enjoyed slurping in fallen moths and crane flies. These fish appeared totally in harmony with their environment, living and feeding both high and low in the water. Then anglers found them, and within two weeks the fish were no longer seen on the surface.

▲ **SURFACE FEEDING** This Spanish barbel loved cavorting on the surface, unafraid, feeding heavily in the surface film on mayflies, sedges, grasshoppers and even, when they were prolific, buzzers. This fish's confidence was misplaced, however, as it was easily caught on a floating dog biscuit.

◀ **CO-OPERATION** As mentioned above, working together is not unique to barbel; sea lampreys, too, will collaborate to move rocks when they are nest digging. This pair – each almost three feet long – was photo-graphed in June after they had swum sixty miles upriver from the sea to spawn. They are excavating a nest around six feet across and eighteen inches deep, into which the female will lay her eggs.

FISHING FOR BARBEL

I hope that the preceding photographs have made you think about the barbel as a complex creature. It is easy to underestimate them, to think of them as 'mere' fish, but, by some means or another, they do learn from unpleasant experiences and become more wary and more difficult to catch. This really is where underwater observation comes in – you can see close up how tackle and bait behave. You can also gauge a barbel's reaction to anything new or suspicious in its orbit. In underwater life, nothing acts as it does in a diagram on the ordered page. You can sit back thinking you have the perfect rig but, believe me, it can look quite ridiculous down there on the river-bed. If there is any one golden rule, it is to make your terminal tackle as simple and straightforward as possible; the more complex, the greater the chance of a tangle; the more components, the greater the risk of discovery.

▲ **FEEDER PROBLEMS** Swim feeders still result in the downfall of many barbel, but be aware of the noise they make on entry. Leave the feeder in longer than normal in order to allow the barbel to gain confidence.

Wading

Whenever possible, it really does pay dividends to get into the water and wade as close to your fish as you can without spooking them. Wading gives all manner of advantages. Firstly, you can often see the fish much more distinctly and this helps when it comes to placing the bait. Secondly, the closer you are, the better you can control your presentation and your tackle. Thirdly, let's look at sheer enjoyment. When wading, you are part of the river and as close to being a barbel as you'll ever get! You'll also get a better idea of the current and feel of the river.

However, you must never take risks or wade any deeper than you feel comfortable with, and never wade into a current that makes you feel uneasy.

Make sure that your wading boots are good and stout, with a sure-grip sole. Always make sure that you have a good, safe, comfortable stance before fishing; don't balance on rocks or anywhere with a slippery surface.

◀ **ATTRACTING FISH** Wading often helps stimulate a swim. Here you see a cloud of silt stirred up by the wading boot. That silt cloud may attract shoals of small fish, whose excitement, in turn, may send ripples of anticipation down the swim. Barbel definitely pick up on this whole feeding frenzy. Also, dribbles of bait from your pouch will move slowly down with the current sending out enticing flavours.

◀ **FALLING SHADOW** You must be particularly aware of your shadow. Of course it's best to fish with the sun behind you so that you can see clearly through the water, particularly if you are wearing Polaroids. However, when you are out in the water you can't make use of bankside vegetation to break up your shadow and this is the result. There is no easy solution, but if you move gently enough, fish will gradually come to accept your shadow, even in comparatively shallow, clear water. Never move with haste.

Bait Presentation

After watching hundreds of barbel baits in action, both in mid-water and on the bottom, I can safely say that many of them don't behave in a way that the angler expects them to. Diagrams in books and magazines may well show the bait and terminal rig lying together in nice, neat patterns, but what these diagrams overlook is the effect of currents, the push of water, the effect of flashes of sunlight and all those things that disrupt the best laid plans of barbel anglers.

If barbel have never been fished for before, it may take you a little while to wean them onto any bait. Barbel that have been pressured in the past are an even harder proposition. Remember that anything that reflects surface brightness, such as a shiny leger weight, will be treated with caution until dusk falls. Another tip is to use pellets for barbel, as these can make a good, clean alternative to particles such as sweetcorn or maggots that become 'blown' on some waters.

Fish close in when the water is dirty, preferably in slacker areas where there is less suspended matter in mid-water. Beware of weeds and leaves getting caught in your line and spoiling your presentation. Think hard about your bait, hooking technique, lead, hook length and exactly where you're going to put all this in any given swim. Barbel will quickly react when they feel a line in mid-water or see a rig that displays a bait in an unnatural fashion.

▶ **A Stark Bait** If barbel are pressured to any degree, then it's almost certain that a single bait lying in an exposed position like this will be treated with the greatest of suspicion. It might be taken, but the chances are that it will be inspected several times by individual fish, often over a period of an hour or more. Don't be in a hurry to recast if this is your approach.

▶ **A 'Merged' Bait** You can certainly expect a quicker bite if your bait is placed amongst free offerings around and about. I've also come to the conclusion that a limited amount of ground bait is also a good idea, as this can often help mask terminal tackle, leads and lines. It also puffs up enticingly when a barbel comes close and begins to stir the water with those powerful pectorals.

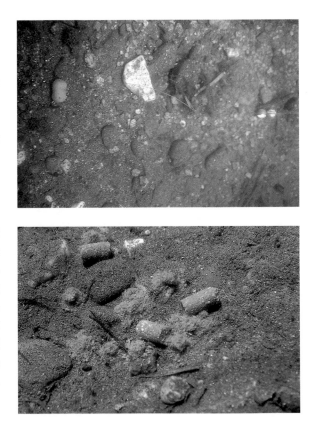

◀ **THE EFFECT OF LIGHT** This picture was taken about five-and-a-half feet beneath the surface of a clear barbel river. Some things about the presentation are good, especially the terminal gear lying on soft weed. But look at the effect of sunlight on the SSG shot and the parts of the exposed hook – to say they glint is an understatement. Think about using a less shiny weight and a smaller hook completely buried in the corn.

◀ **THE FLAT LEAD** I do like the look of flat leads when I see them, like this one, five or six feet down. It appears to me and, I'm sure, also to the barbel, that they stand out much less obviously than bigger bullets or, especially, feeders. Once again, a lot of this is to do with the light. The flat lead snuggles into the silt and looks like any other stone.

◀ **THE ISOLATED BAIT** This is another example of a bait sticking out like a sore thumb. I've now switched heavily onto pellets, but the pellet has to be positioned correctly. Look at it here. In this crystal-clear water the pellet stands out almost obscenely; even the minnows keep away from it.

▶ **COVER** This time the bait has rolled down the sand and is much closer to the relatively sparse vegetation. Here, the minnows feel much more confident pecking at it. It will be in an area similar to this that barbel, too, will accept a bait more readily.

▶ **THE TROUGH** If you can get your bait into one of the mini troughs that many barbel swims are riddled with, then you'll be in business. With the help of the current, the bait will drift down until it catches in a particular, tight, attractive area. It's in these places that the barbel feed hard – you will see that even the minnows keep away from such areas out of fear of being sucked in along with the pellets.

▶ **THE WASHING-LINE EFFECT** Accurate, tight bait presentation is especially difficult after a flood or in the autumn months. Weed and leaves become dislodged and float downstream until they cling to your line. Weed attracts weed and soon the line is bowed and your bait is pulled out of position. The weed also highlights the presence of the line itself.

◄ **In the Swim** This attractive seven-pound barbel has entered a swim around four-and-a-half to five feet deep and is busy hoovering-up pellets. The water is not too clear, the day is overcast and the fish looks reasonably confident, especially as there are sparse weed beds around. Barbel do not like thick silt or mud; they will feed over clean sand and gravel but adore plentiful small stones that they can suck around and grub over.

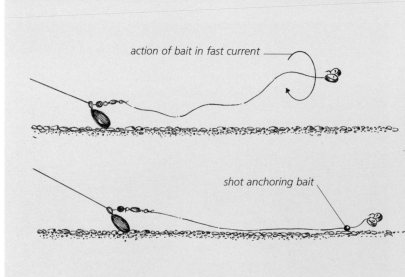

◄ **Alarmed** The pectorals flay out wide and the dorsal fin stands up proud. The fish is very close to a terminal rig and there's clearly something wrong. Barbel also show this type of reaction when they rub against the line. They may veer off or, more commonly, just drift away.

action of bait in fast current

shot anchoring bait

Fast Water Problems

Any fish can spot an unnatural-looking bait, and the movement of the food item in the water can be a crucial factor. In a strong-flowing river, a light bait, such as sweetcorn, is likely to be swung about in the current and may even 'helicopter' – spin wildly at the end of the line. A single shot pinched onto the line close to the bait will keep the bait down and increase the chances of a fish treating it as part of its natural food supply.

Barbel on the Fly

These shots were taken in Spain. I truly believe that the more we experiment with barbel-fishing techniques, the greater the challenge and satisfaction. Although these shots were taken in warm, clear water, you can catch barbel on the nymph in many other countries. I first saw it practised in the Czech Republic where the method was taught to me by Franta, a member of the Czech national team. Since then, I've had a good few barbel on nymphs in the UK, and I know of others who have also succeeded. It's not too difficult – you just need belief.

Water type is important – ideally you need a steadily paced piece of water, no deeper than five feet, for the nymph method to work properly. Standard trout gear will do, with a six-pound tippet. Some flies simply won't be acceptable, but if you keep changing, you will most likely hit on a successful pattern. Experiment with all manner of nymph patterns. The best sizes appear to be tied to anything between a size six and twelve. Let the flies – a team of two or three nymphs works well – drift close to the river-bed and watch a strike indicator for a take. Fish with confidence. It's important to realize that barbel have fed on all manner of nymphs for thousands of years before we appeared with our maggots, hemp and corn.

▶ **SIGHTING FISH** You need to be able to see fish in the swim in front of you, partly for confidence, but also to gauge their reaction to the various flies. Wading will help you to get closer to the fish, as well as helping you to control your line better.

▶ **THE FLY IN THE WATER** You will need plenty of weight on a fly to get it down to the bottom of the water, which is where barbel generally pick them up.

◄ **THE STRIKE** Barbel will suck in an artificial nymph with amazing speed and eject it just as quickly. So, watch the fly if you can, as well as your leader or a strike indicator of some description. Strike quickly and cleanly at anything you think is suspicious and, eventually, you will be amazed when your first barbel takes. Don't fish at too great a distance as you won't be able to see the take, control the fly or set the hook fast enough if a take occurs. Whenever possible, use a floating line.

◄ **THE BATTLE** You'll find that barbel, even ones like this comparatively small fish, fight much better on fly tackle than they do on normal coarse gear. Take your time, but don't allow the fish to dictate the battle. Make sure you've got plenty of backing under your fly line, and be prepared to follow the fish if necessary… barbel of eight pounds plus will generally take all the line and a good deal of the backing, and it's difficult to bring them back against the current on light fly gear.

◄ **FIRMLY HOOKED** Creatures similar to this artificial fly make up the basic diet of any barbel and will be accepted readily. Sometimes you need to work the fly just a little bit. At others times simply let it drift in the current. It's impossible to be dogmatic about technique as not enough work has yet been done on this fascinating subject.

BARBEL CARE AND CONSERVATION

What I have to say about consideration for the welfare of barbel applies equally to every species. Through years of diving I have become convinced that fish are far less tough than anglers consider. For example, it's quite obvious that fish that have been caught and returned, but not kept in a net, have suffered trauma to some degree. Also, you'd be surprised how long wounds inflicted during capture take to heal. Barbel are especially vulnerable to damage and danger; they fight valiantly, using up great reserves of energy. They are also frequently fighting against the current of the river as well as the strain of your tackle, and that greatly increases the exhaustion factor. Also, as barbel are often caught in the warmest weather, the lack of oxygen does nothing to aid a quick recovery. So, all in all, take the greatest care of your barbel.

▲ **To the Bankside** Can there be a more lovely sight than a barbel caught in the sunlight? Be aware, however, that as soon as the fish leaves the water those glistening scales dry out perilously quickly.

The Barbel Fight

Quite rightly the barbel is revered as one of the great fighters of fresh water, and newcomers to the barbel scene are often shell-shocked by the power and resilience a barbel will show. But what goes on unseen while you are fighting that barbel? Why is a barbel so special? Well, it may well be its perfect balance, large fins and muscular body, which combine to make it one amazing, rippling, fighting machine.

A reminder: many barbel are lost right at the end of the fight as the angler relaxes. To avoid this occurring, always ensure that the reel's clutch is set to give line to a last run and move the fish to the net slowly and gently so that it is not further alarmed.

◀ **POWER** Here you can see a barbel of close on nine pounds grudgingly prised from the bottom towards the surface. Not for long. Watch how the body arches and the fins flair. We are keen to talk about the size of the barbel's pectorals but look, too, at those pelvic fins and even the large anal fin. Within a split second of taking this shot, the barbel nose-dived and plunged irresistibly back to the river-bed.

◀ **THE PROPELLER** I love this shot I took of a barbel midway through a fight. Just look at the great sweep of that tail as it powers the fish away from danger. Note, too, how the whole body works in one sinuous whiplash movement.

▶ **THE LAST SURGE** You know how it is… you've been playing a barbel for ten minutes – although it seems like more – and then you get the fish to the surface, where it eyes you cautiously. With most other fish the battle is now over, but not with the barbel. The view of the terrestrial world spurs it into a last-gasp effort and, with that mighty tail, it slaps the surface and powers off yet again. This is the moment when you don't want that clutch to be set too tight.

▶ **A FLASH OF LIGHT** This is what you see from below when the barbel is finally beaten and guided into the waiting net. It's interesting, too, that this is the moment that the light above the surface catches the scales of any fish most brightly… a key, perhaps, to those frequent, last-minute pike attacks on your catch.

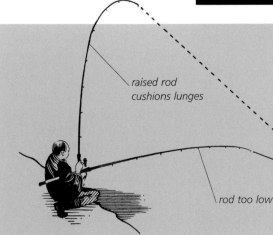

raised rod cushions lunges

rod too low

End of the Battle

The final moments of the fight with a barbel can be crucial – really make or break. Remember that the fish will nearly always make a last powerful run, and make sure you are well prepared for this eventuality. Don't have your clutch set too tight or the moving fish will be unable to take line. Don't lower your rod too close to the water or you will lose its ability to cushion the line.

Landing the Barbel

There is no doubt that removing the fish bodily from the water onto the side of the bank is one of the most stressful elements of the whole catching process. The photographs that appear here show how I, ideally, like to treat any barbel that I catch... and that's by not removing them from the water at all, at any single stage. Believe me, fish recover much more quickly when they are kept in the water throughout the whole unhooking process.

The technique shown in the pictures below is the most fish-friendly method of dealing with fish after the fight. Obviously, however, it can only be carried out in those circumstances where you can wade or at least get right to the water-line in complete safety. Don't try it in swollen water or on steep, slippery banks. The fish is a very important creature, but the angler's safety is paramount.

◀ **BATTLE OVER** The barbel is now secure in the net, which is deep and soft meshed. The fish is calm, the fight is over and it's almost as though it accepts its fate – while in the water, that is.

◀ **UNHOOKING** Lift the barbel to the water-line so that the hook, often barbless, can be slipped from the lip with that pair of forceps that you should always carry clipped to your lapel. Even at this stage the fish is still largely in the water, with the river still coursing through its gills.

▶ **RELEASING YOUR CATCH** Kneel in the water and guide the fish from the net, still keeping hold of it with both hands. This is vitally important: if you don't keep control at this stage the barbel can wriggle free only to find the current is too strong for it. At this point it could easily drift from sight and turn over in the current.

▶ **TAKING IN AIR** As you begin to feel power return to the barbel, and once you are sure it will not keel over in the water if it is left unsupported, then you can hold it with one hand back towards the tail. Note, too, that bubble of oxygen escaping from the gills; air was gulped just in those few seconds that the fish was held on the water-line. Imagine how much more air is taken on board if the fish is physically taken from the water for any length of time.

▶ **COMPLETE RETURN OF POWER** This fish – a Spanish barbel, in fact – is now working its body dynamically, totally ready to be let free. The fish has made its own mind up and off it goes, totally safe and not unduly stressed.

Care at the Bankside

There are times when you will want a quick photograph of a barbel out of its watery home. Or, perhaps, the fish is very large and you want to weigh it. There are numerous reasons for taking a barbel from the river, but do make sure the reason is a good one, and keep the period that the fish is actually out in the air to a very minimum. If you do require to get you and your friends' faces in a photo with your catch, remember it is up to you to go to the fish rather than vice versa, so that the time the fish is out of the water is reduced. I believe that it is especially important not to take the barbel any real distance from the water – get that fish back as soon as you can.

▲ **BARBEL ON RANUNCULUS** This shows a barbel in its natural environment, resting on the weed that it lives amongst. The limpid nature of the fish is also emphasized as the water brushes its flanks.

◀ **A TEAM PHOTOGRAPH** Note that the barbel here is held over the landing net in case it should struggle and fall helpless into the current. It is also held over the water so that it won't crash onto sand, gravel or rock.

▶ **BE CAREFUL** Now these are three special shots because they are a lasting record of a boy's first barbel, caught under the care and supervision of his father. A moment that all the family will be proud of for ever. Note here the concentration on Jack's face as his father, Tony, steadies the fish in preparation for the photograph.

▶ **HOLD STEADY** Jack's brother, Christopher, is also standing by in case Jack or Tony lose their grip. All three made sure their hands were glistening wet before touching the fish. In an ideal world, I would like to have seen an unhooking mat brought into operation at this stage, but the grass was very thick, lush and damp. The barbel has been out of the water less than 30 seconds at this stage.

▶ **SPEED IS OF THE ESSENCE** Tony, Jack, Christopher and the barbel look up for two or three very quick photographs. I had already made sure that my camera was switched on, focused and ready to go, and the barbel was back in the water just 52 seconds after being taken from the water.

FISHING FOR BIG-WATER CARP

Big-water carp fishing has been the rock 'n' roll of the sport for the past twenty years, with most attention focusing on France and several Central and Eastern European waters. Spain, by comparison, has been largely overlooked. The common impression is that there are plenty of twenty- and thirty-pound fish in Spain but nothing much bigger. The following pictures were taken in and around a very large water in central Spain, and while I was here I saw some very big fish, deep down in the crystal-clear water. It's sometimes difficult to estimate the size of fish when you are diving, but they certainly appeared much larger than those that I saw caught.

A quick tip: with long-distance casting it is very easy for your terminal tangle to land in a heap. A few turns of the reel handle as the rig is sinking helps straighten everything out before it lands. If you try to haul things into shape once the rig has already hit bottom, then you run the risk of pulling the bait into weed or a snag. Fish as tightly and as directly as you can and you'll see a real difference in your catch rate.

◀ **ACCURACY** It is essential to have a marker indicating where you have laid your bed of bait. On very large waters with little surface detail, it is easy to be rod lengths away from the target.

Boily Presentation

When you venture into the depths, you can see that certain rigs simply do not look right at all. Also, the casting process itself means that terminal tackle doesn't lie as it is supposed to. Once again, sunlight and water clarity simply combine to highlight any mistakes in the set up. No surprise, therefore, that murky water and/or night fishing often pay dividends.

On large waters the strength of the underwater currents can be immense, especially after periods of strong wind. Take this into account when baiting up and casting, particularly if the swim is a deep one. Remember that the tow of the water can easily drift both baits and free offerings many yards from where you would expect them to land. Think, too, of the pressure of the undertows on your long line leading from the bank all the way to the bait: tighten up carefully and use as thin a line as is safe for the fish. Long-distance work makes many demands, so consider any potential problems carefully.

Also, always be sure to remember the importance of camouflage, and endeavour to match the hook and hook link material with the type of bottom that dominates your chosen swim.

▶ **THE PVA STRINGER** This is PVA mesh tape, which is easy to use. As it is a mesh, you simply pass the hook point through the holes, so there is no need to tie any knots. The stringer of course allows for very tight baiting even at long range.

▶ **SEPARATION** Here, you can see that the mesh has just about given way and the boilies are moving apart – the bottom ones are actually rolling off down the gravel slope, and will continue to do so for another two to three feet. Tight baiting isn't always as easy as you would think.

▶ **A FATAL FLAW** Braid hook length can merge totally with the colour of the lake bed. Full marks so far, but just look at the hook. This photograph was taken about eight feet down on a very hot day and the hook itself is highlighted by the bright sun; from certain angles it really shines like a beacon… not a good idea. Constantly think of camouflage for everything – even hooks.

◀ **THE GREED FACTOR** A good example of a pop-up rig. Instead of using a counter-balance, such as a split shot or heavy metal putty, you can also use a non pop-up bait of the same size to counter-balance and also to appeal to the greed factor. Big fish, especially, often like a set-up such as this as they can, quite literally, get two for the price of one suck! Moreover, it looks very good when fish are in the swim as both the baits hover and bounce in the currents created.

◀ **THE ANTI-EJECT RIG** Several points to note here. Look at the camo hook. This rig also incorporates heavy metal putty as the counter-balance. The hook has been coated green so it merges with the weed background. The bait is attached to a small rig ring that runs along a stiff loop of mono attached to the outer edge of the hook; this allows the boily independent movement, which – in theory – makes it more difficult for a suspicious fish to eject the hook from its mouth.

▲ **THE PVA BAG** A PVA bag allows us to introduce free offerings of many different types and sizes, but it is important that the chosen bait is dry. We can also introduce our baited rig, including the lead set-up, ensuring accurate baiting and tangle-free presentation. PVA bags are ideal in weedy swims as they drift slowly down, land on top of the weed and then dissolve there, avoiding your rig being pulled rapidly through the weed.

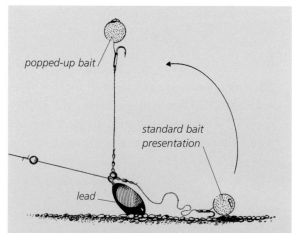

popped-up bait

standard bait presentation

lead

Popping It Up

A buoyant bait drifts tantalizingly in the underwater currents created by feeding fish. It is a particularly useful ploy to use over dirty or weedy bottoms. Remember natural baits work well popped up: try a lively lobworm suspended by a polystyrene ball.

Catch and Release

These shots were taken throughout a blissful session on a mammoth Spanish lake in the month of June. The water was crystal clear and wonderfully warm, with a bright sun overhead – ideal for diving and photography. And the carp were obliging; perhaps because angling pressure had been slight, they were easy to approach and to catch.

The pop-up bait was successful in this case. It's surprising to what degree those underwater currents can manipulate a well popped-up bait, making it wave and dance just off the bottom to catch the eye of a hungry fish.

As the carp proved difficult to land on the bank, a dinghy was used to net the catch. However, it's one thing to land a carp in a boat but it's another thing entirely to release a fish from one. You are much better rowing back to the shallows, where you can slip over the side to join the fish and support it until it is strong enough to swim back to the depths.

▶ **THE POP-UP** This extravagant pop-up proves irresistible to a lovely Spanish mirror. Normally, you might expect such an obtrusive bait in so open a piece of ground to send off warning signals, but this big, hungry fish homes straight in.

▶ **COMING CLOSE** When you're fishing at long range, the fight with a big carp is strangely cushioned by both the rod and the stretch in the line. However, get close to the fighting fish and you'll be awed by its power and the way its body spins and manoeuvres in continuous attempts to throw the hook.

▲ THE BOAT When there are hazards between the bank and the catch, as in this case, dinghies can be used. With each hooked fish, simply ride out clear of the weed so that the carp can be netted with no danger of snagging. This is, in reality, a two-man job. Be very careful of playing a fish and controlling a boat at the same time, especially in the darkness or if there's a wind. In either of these cases, it is extremely foolhardy to go out without a buoyancy aid, especially if the water is at all cold. Hypothermia can set in far faster than you would think.

◀ THE RELEASE In warm water, which holds less oxygen, a long fight takes a great deal out of a carp, and it's almost invariably necessary to nurse it back to full strength before releasing it. This should be a period to enjoy, allowing the beauty of the fish to wash over you, enhancing the satisfaction of a challenge met and overcome.

CARP OBSERVATIONS

It's great to get up close and personal with fish, and carp, partly because of their size and well-defined habits, are ideal targets. They are also interesting because they have individual characteristics. To make any real study of carp, you need relatively clear water that is not too deep and gives plenty of good vantage points. Obviously you need Polaroids, but I would also stress that a pair of good binoculars is critical. Viewing a carp through binoculars as it swims around your baited area is like watching fish on television – you are there, almost swimming with it. Make sure that you also have plenty of time. Don't rush carp observations because, if you do, you'll very probably come to the wrong conclusions. So have patience, lie low, watch everything that's going on like a hawk and you will soon begin to learn a huge amount more about carp than you ever thought possible.

▲ **A CARPER'S DREAM** The very essence of the perfect carp-stalking water – clear and shallow – and think of the joys of spotting fish from the regal comfort of the boathouse balcony.

Estate Lake Carp

I'm the first to admit that the quieter the water, the more satisfactory the likely end result. Stalking carp visually is not best done on crowded waters or ones that are heavily clouded. However, on any water I maintain that a few sessions simply watching will provide good results when it comes to catching carp.

In an ideal world, where there are relatively quiet waters, you'll nearly always find that carp love to feed and patrol the margins. That doesn't mean for a second that you won't find them out in the main body of the lake, but it's the margins that continually prove the magnet. In large part, this is due to the amount of food in the shallows, which are warmed by the sun and often stirred up by drinking cattle.

◀ THE MARGINS Here you can see a couple of fish bubbling frantically just a rod length from the bank, a sight common to this lake and many other estate pools that I know well.

◀ BANK PATROL Even if the fish aren't feeding close to the bank, you will often see them moving around here. Since spending a lot of time under the water, I have certain theories about this. The margins of many estate lakes are well trodden by cattle as they come down to drink, and I believe that their constant wading clears the silt off the gravel and creates a very fertile food source, plus their dung just has to help the bloodworm to breed in lavish amounts!

▶ **SPAWNING** Ninety times out of a hundred, it's the margins that see carp spawning. It's a good idea to get out to the lake when the carp do spawn because it really gives an idea of the maximum potential of the fish present. When they are spawning, you can get very close to the carp indeed. In fact, on occasions, I've actually had to lift carp back into the lake that have been hurled from the water in the throes of passion!

▶ **FEEDERS** You can see fish moving very close in under the shadow of some overhanging trees. These fish are definitely feeding: you can tell by the slow speed at which they are travelling and because they are very close to the bottom. There's no doubt that a bed of particles will pull down a couple of fish acting in this way. Modern carp pellets are excellent, and it's hard to beat maggots and casters.

▶ **TAKING IT EASY** A large carp is resting in a dense weed bed. To catch this somnolent fish find the largest lobworm you can and nip off the tail and head so that it can't burrow into the weeds. Cast the lobworm way beyond the carp and slowly retrieve it inch by inch until it's hanging in open water, close to the carp's head. Watch for a take; the line will only move an inch or two as the carp sucks in the worm. Strike quickly.

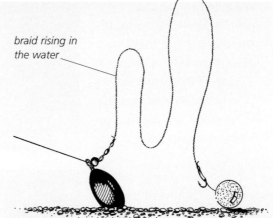

braid rising in the water

▲ **Good Gear** Okay, this all looks a bit twee and traditional but, believe me, it's gear that works. Firstly, in the right circumstances, you can't beat a float as an indicator. This isn't always the case, but if you want to introduce a bait very lightly without a heavy lead, then it's ideal. And the centre pin? For close-in work they are brilliant, and if you haven't played a big carp off a centre pin then you've missed out on one of the great angling experiences. As there isn't any gearing, you are playing the fish directly off the reel and the sensation is much more violent and raw. As for the old cane rod? Well, it's a Mark IV, and what was good enough for the one-time record carp is certainly good enough for me. In fact, for close-in work, I reckon a cane rod like this is probably the best tool still on the market. It's soft and very forgiving, and you can wind it right round past its test curve without pulling a hook. It's heavy, but you're not holding it for long, and you can just lay it on the grass or in the rushes until a carp approaches.

Presentation Problems

Always be aware of how quickly carp learn. An obvious giveaway is a braid hook length that becomes buoyant and curls up round the bait. Go for a heavier braid or weight it to the bottom. Think, too, about the line from the lead to the rod, as this can be very obvious to the fish. Back leading can prove invaluable in clear water or where the carp have learned to feel for line.

Winter Branches

Come winter and nearly every carp I've come up against has been next to cover. Branches are a favourite, but if the lake has lily beds, you'll find carp close in among the died-back roots. I'm not sure quite why carp and shelter go so closely together – perhaps it's something to do with the darker light values or perhaps the water is slightly warmer in these places.

Remember that lakes can be far clearer in winter than in the summer. Winter sunlight can make you feel that you are diving encased in a diamond, and I've seen carp veer away from a float two, if not three, yards away. They are also likely to be much more aware of line in the mid-water... two strong reasons to go for back-leaded legering gear.

▶ **HEAVY FEEDING** The lake was coloured and the weather wet and mild, definitely putting the carp on the feed. There were several fish close to the margins under fallen trees and I decided to go for them with bloodworm. I mixed these with ground bait and threw several balls into the area. The result was cataclysmic. The carp fed greedily. The successful hook bait proved to be a couple of brandlings on a size ten and the float simply dived each time.

▶ **LEGER TIME** I would not have got away with the float in water as clear as this. I think you've got to go back to the lead to catch fish like these in real clear-water situations.

Sweetcorn Strategies

Particles, sweetcorn in particular, really exploded out of the European carp scene in the 1960s and 1970s, but, since the 1980s, in the UK at least, they have become over-used. Carp can be suspicious of corn and other particles as a result, but the fact remains that they do love them.

With careful presentation, therefore, even corn can still prove to be a winner. Try experimenting with baits and different set-ups in shallow water and see for yourself what looks right.

◀ **GUZZLER** This shot of a carp shovelling in sweetcorn was taken in a big European lake where even my presence couldn't put the fish off. It was good to be reassured about the use of corn, seeing just how much carp love it. I have no doubt that the slight clouding of the water also encouraged the fish.

◀ **FAR TOO OBVIOUS** This used to be my standard rig back in the 1970s… a couple of grains of sweetcorn on a size eight, for example, with the requisite amount of SSG to make the casting distance. But, looking at it in situ, you can see why it wouldn't catch many wised-up carp these days. Believe me, the carp would see those shot just as easily as the grains of corn themselves and would have nothing to do with a set-up that is so basic.

▶ **Mid-water Cruisers** The corn – this time on braid – is draped down the side of a large rock. This gives it a real chance of being picked off by mid-water cruisers – fish that keep to one level as they swim. When they come across food at that level, they're likely to suck it in, so if a carp swimming four or five feet off the bottom passes this rock and comes eye-to-eye with the corn, then it will be taken. If the corn is higher up the rock or on the bottom, it is likely to be ignored.

▶ **Moving On** From what I've witnessed, corn presented like this stands a real chance of being taken. The bait is attractive, and coloured corn can make quite a difference. What makes it a real winner, though, is the way the braid is lying inconspicuously against the rock. Carp are neurotically afraid of any line – braid or mono – that is evident in mid-water; if you can lay it hard on the bottom or against a rock like this, then you've got a real chance.

▶ **Good Positioning** Again, there's a good possibility that this carp will be caught. The blocks behind the fish help to break up the profile of the line. Also, if a carp has to negotiate snags on a rocky bottom, then it's got less of an eye open for the giveaway signs of an angler's tackle. Of course, the great problem for any angler on the bank is knowing how to place a bait as accurately as this, especially at distance. Obviously, an angler on a vast gravel pit can't cast over a hundred yards and know exactly how his bait is lying on the bed. Try to get afloat in conditions of good visibility, and make a real effort to get some impression of the ground you are fishing over.

◀ **POP-UPS** This pop-up was cast out some fifty yards away, and it has landed about ten feet down in a crystal lake on a very bright day. You can even see the shadow the bait creates on the sandy gravel beneath it. Although it is a text-book set-up in many ways, the angler may still be sitting there without a bite. For fish that are at all pressured, a bait as stark as this just isn't a realistic option.

◀ **PVA** If, however, you incorporate a pop-up such as this in a PVA bag filled with soft pellets, ground bait or anything that forms a cloud, then you're in with some sort of a chance. Of course, there are problems. The splash as the bag enters the water can really spook fish over a wide area. You will probably need heavier main line if you're casting heavy weights and this cuts down on distance. Accuracy becomes more problematic, too, as the bag is apt to be caught by crosswinds in flight.

◀ **CREATE YOUR OWN CLOUD** If I'm right and presentation is a great deal of the game, then it's probably worth taking the risk. You'll see how the PVA bag has pretty well melted and the bait inside is blurring the disastrous impact of the terminal tackle very nicely indeed. A further bonus would be if small fish came in to peck at the bait particles – another way to lure carp into a position where they're eminently catchable.

▶ **BAY OF PLENTY** I had realized that this bay, situated as it is towards the eastern end of a large lake, had been catching the force of a steady westerly breeze for several days. As I had hoped and expected, large numbers of carp had moved into the area, feeding close in on the mountain of insect life that had drifted into the bay's margins. A delicate presentation was called for, and I favoured a float. However, note how I have left the float uncocked. A cocked float is much more obtrusive from below. As it is, the float could be a twig drifting in the wind.

▶ **SUCCESS** I'm not a great fan of hats – too hot and stuffy – but here the broad peak kept the bright light off my eyes so that my Polaroid glasses could function more clearly. I picked up some ten or so fish during the first day and a half, but then it became obvious that the carp were becoming more and more aware of the line from the float to the bait. In the end, I was forced to light leger, but after two more fish the carp left the bay completely.

Feeding Observations

This is really what we want to see – carp heavily on the feed, oblivious to our terminal tackle, laying themselves open to being caught. Watching feeding carp is really quite an experience. You suddenly realize just how big and how muscular carp are, and what power they can generate. You can also appreciate their colours and their strength as they tip and plough into the bottom, pushing aside large stones or fallen branches. It's no surprise that heavily-feeding fish can make quite a crater in the lake-bed in just a short time. In fact, where the bed is reasonably soft, feeding hollows of nearly a foot in depth are not uncommon.

There's no doubt as to why murky-water carp are easier to catch than clear-water fish: no matter how coloured the water, the carp will sense or smell the bait, while the terminal gear and the line to it are much more difficult to pick out and avoid.

▲ **Tail Power** The rudder is the real driving force behind the carp, but all the fins help propel it into the bottom gravel and stone. The currents that a carp generates are very noticeable and a group of big fish can create a mini tidal wave.

▲ **PERFECTION** It's exactly this type of scenario that makes a take very likely indeed. First, you've got a hard-feeding fish. Second, you've got water that's either cloudy or has been made cloudy by the carp's feeding aggression. Lastly, you've got healthy undergrowth on the bottom, which goes a long way to masking any careless terminal rig.

▲ **ON THE PROWL** The body language of these two common carp is absolutely unmistakable. They are moving in unison through clear water, some three feet deep, both of them on the search for food. Look how their bodies are curved as they sweep their heads from side to side, looking for bloodworm, snail or anything else that attracts.

▲ **WARY** This is a fascinating piece of action. The carp knows there's bait about but it's very wary. Look at the braid, which is leading down from the lily stem towards a boily that is just visible in the bottom left-hand corner. The line has been in the water half an hour and has become highlighted by tiny air bubbles that have attached themselves to the line, and these are lit up by the sun on the water.

Getting It Right

Okay, I'm making a lot of this, but if line in mid-water is glaringly obvious to me then it certainly is to the carp, and that is very much supported by what I'm witnessing from below. Also, a carp will often watch a bait for minutes, if not hours, on end waiting for it to be moved or for anything to betray it. If you are not catching, then think again about your bait, rig and presentation.

a small weight on the line set back from the leger weight keeps the line on the bottom

▶ **RUDDY CHEEK** So what happens next? The carp moves away a little and other smaller fish come in, attracted by the smells of the bait. In particular, a clutch of small rudd appears and begins to peck at the loose offerings around the bait. The carp watches this, becomes agitated and makes a return.

▲ **THE BULLY** Carp are hungry beasts and fearful of losing any potential feast. Although it is still wary of the angler's trap, the appearance of those rudd has galvanized the carp into a display of violent feeding behaviour. Also, of course, the more the bottom is stirred up, the more the water colours and the less visible the braid and terminal rig become.

FISHING ROACH RIVERS

It's high summer and the river is running warm and crystal clear; there is heavy weed growth – water cabbages in particular – but in between lie patches of clear sand and gravel where it is possible to watch large shoals of roach as they glide through the polished water. The fish are feeding almost constantly on the huge variety of insects that the river harbours during the warmer summer months. This is the River Wensum, once by far the best river for roach in eastern England until it fell on hard times in the 1970s and '80s. The rumour is, however, that sensitive river management by the Environment Agency has seen huge improvements and the smaller fish have come back in droves. There truly has been a big turn around in recent years, and a much more enlightened bureaucratic approach could lead to a boom time in just a few years.

▲ RIVER MANAGEMENT The mills are very important to the well-being of lowland rivers. Sensitive sluice gate management is vital to prevent over-rapid run-off, which can dislodge whole generations of small fish.

Centre Pin and Boat

A nostalgic return to an idyllic past? Not a bit of it. The boat is absolutely essential to get us upstream to the place where most of the roach are feeding, among underwater cabbages alongside banks, yards deep in impenetrable reed beds. We see some roach rising to sip in struggling sedge flies and the whole impression is of a river teeming with life, well on the way to a full recovery. As for the centre pin? Well, a better tool for trotting has never been created. Control of the line and float is perfect and, without a bail arm, an instant strike can be made.

▲ THE BOAT A half-mile row sees the boys at the top of a fabulous glide. They've fed in half a bucket of loose mash and are putting up their gear. Soon, they'll anchor the boat out across the river so that they can trot the stream with perfect, direct control. The river here is about seven feet deep and the cabbage beds rise up to just over the mid-water mark.

▶ THE PIN Even though the river isn't very swift here, there is still just enough current to lift line from the pin without Alex having to raise a finger to help. If he wants to stop the float and raise the bait – a piece of breadflake – all he has to do is dab the spool rim with his finger. At the end of an unsuccessful trot down he can bat the gear back with the palm of his hand, flicking the spool just as quickly as any man can reel in with a fixed-spool reel. If the float does dip and a roach is on, the strike is made and you're immediately playing the fish without any need to click over a bail arm.

Life Among the Cabbages

Deep dredging as a tool of river management was initiated in the UK shortly after the Second World War. Unfortunately, it devastated not only the river-bed but also bankside vegetation. Fish, flora and fauna all suffered massively. Gradually, the Environment Agency, at least in south-east England, has phased out the practice, sending it back into the mists where it belongs. Happily, the River Wensum is already beginning to show the benefits.

The return of the roach has benefited the whole food chain. Pike are next on the ladder, and it's noticeable that the numbers and average sizes have risen over the past few years. Keep your eye out for river-bank wildlife too.

◀ ROACH IN SUNLIGHT While Alex prepared to start running through his float, I was able to sink into the water and see just how many pristine, scale-perfect, young roach were swimming in the area. These fish, I guess, weigh between four and twelve ounces and are probably between two and four years of age. If the gods are kind to them, in three or four more years, many of them will be true specimens.

◀ THE PREDATOR Most of the pike I saw that day were down deep, well hidden in the cabbage beds, digesting food and content to let the day pass them by. This fish, around five or six pounds, however, is quite obviously on the prowl. And it didn't particularly like the look of me!

▶ **THE PREDATOR BECOMES PREY**
For many years, otters were virtually driven from the Wensum valley simply because there wasn't enough food for them to survive. Now there are several otters working the upper and middle river, and it's not unusual to find their droppings and prints in any soft, muddy area. Get out early and you might be lucky enough to see them hunting or whistling to their young.

▶ **RATTY** This is a fantastic sight. Ratty – the water vole – in its full pomp, sitting and eating a reed in the glow of a summer morning. These adorable little creatures have been under severe threat during the past years. Destruction of their habitat – again by the dredger – did them no good whatsoever. And then the appearance of that most loathsome of predators, the mink, tried to do what the digger could not – eradicate the water vole entirely. Now, happily, in small colonies, ratty is returning.

The Float and the Cabbage

It is a fact that the underwater cabbages attract the roach with the shade and food they offer, but trotting through them isn't always easy. The cabbages are not a level playing field, but more like a green, underwater range of mountains.

You want your bait to travel as close to the top of the cabbages as possible, but, if you misjudge the depth, then you will consistently hang up. When you follow a bait downstream you realize that it rarely behaves as textbooks would have us believe. Breadflake, especially, seems to rise and fall of its own volition, and will frequently travel downstream actually above the bottom shot. If you modify your gear a little, by dropping the float down three or four inches, the bait should travel just over the head of the cabbages. Also, if you squeeze a little more air out of the flake before putting it on the hook, it will be less buoyant and will trundle downstream below the bottom shot. Floats are strange things when seen under water, and fish see them very clearly. I remember catching a big, wild carp that had veered away from a traditional float at a shallow local lake; it was only when I tied on a discarded goose feather as a bite indicator that the carp took the bait.

◀ ▼ THE FLAT FLOAT The bait and/or the shot is hung up on a cabbage leaf, and the float is neither allowed to cock nor move off down river. The mobile roach may chance upon the marooned piece of flake, but you can't really explore the river as you'd like to. Here, the breadflake has wedged against a cabbage leaf above the bottom shot and further progress is impossible.

▲ ▶ **ANOTHER GO** The modified rig has the breadflake just flicking the top of the cabbages – ideal. The float is cocked, but the angler isn't adding shot to bury it deeper, because if he did, every time the breadflake brushed a lip of cabbage, the float would drop – increasing the number of abortive strikes.

▶ **LIGHT AND SHADE** Here, you see the dark stem of the float quite obvious against the reflected light of a pad. These roach are young, naive and pretty well unfished for. However, give these fish a few years and a little more wisdom, and a more subtle float approach will probably be necessary. If the fish become very wary, then it is probable that when the water is clear they will only be catchable on a lead.

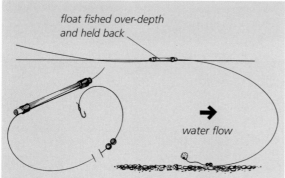

float fished over-depth
and held back

water flow

Stretpegging

This is an old and effective way of catching roach. Use a float attached top and bottom and set it well over-depth – in quick water, twice the depth is not too much. Let the float work its way down the swim, little by little, holding it back for a minute or two before letting it on its way again. This is a good way to search out water, but note the big loop of line that the fish will come to before the bait – often not the best method for clear water.

▲ **SCALE PERFECT** Not a big fish, just a few ounces, but still a beacon of light for the future. It's a long time since flawless roach such as this were seen swimming the River Wensum, and, I gather, many other southern, lowland rivers come to that. A quick trophy shot on the damp and cool of a lily pad and then back it slips to grow, to learn and to become a two-pounder.

FISHING FOR CHUB

I've never done chub justice. When I've wanted barbel… along comes a chub. When I've been obsessed with big roach… along comes a chub. Perhaps it's diving that's enlightened me. The more I've seen chub under water, the more I've come to realize why Izaak Walton called them 'the fearfulest of fishes'.

Chub are fish of infinite variety. You'll find them feeding on just about every possible food source – digging up boulders to get at caddis, slurping fallen moths, chasing elvers. Under water, you begin to realize just how keen their sight and hearing is, and they show endless cunning when faced with anglers' baits. Imagine the scene: I'm lying watching a group of chub some ten feet away; an angler plops in a float or a lead, ten or even twenty yards up river. The chub immediately show unease. If the lead is increased in size or dropped closer, they will bolt. So, try to introduce your hook bait and loose feed as quietly as you can. If you're wading, introduce the feed by hand actually under the water level so there's no noise of its entry. Cast well upstream and let the bait move down towards the fish as silently as possible.

▲ **ALL EYES** Chub are generally shoal fish, and their already keen senses work even more effectively with shared information. Look at those big eyes: no wonder they are hard to fool in clear water.

Chub and Float

A float can be a really useful tool when chub fishing, though most anglers today prefer legering. The great advantage a float gives you is that you can move a bait up to a hundred yards when searching for fish. Also, the bait will creep up to a chub silently without the dreaded splash of the descending leger.

The older and wiser chub become, the more they seek out surface cover and hang underneath it. To get a legered bait close to such fish would be very difficult. You'd have to cast it very close to the branch and that would mean the devastating chub-scaring plop. Far better to use a float to get the bait down past their noses. Running the float as close to the snag as you can. If possible, wade out into mid-river, a long way upstream, to give you a better angle and more control. Lengthen the distance between the float and the bait, so that the float is further off and less easily seen. Free-lining is an excellent tactic for really careful, spooked fish.

▲ **COVER** These particular fish are quite obviously on their guard, hanging close under a branch that's become festooned with passing weed and pieces of rush – any flotsam and jetsam the river pushes towards it. It's a good place for them to garner food as well as feel secure.

◀ **A SORE THUMB** If you let a float travel in open water it will stick out like the proverbial sore thumb – the chub will see it coming at least two to three yards off and either flee or make a big detour. If you are forced to use a float without any cover, try not cocking it but let it drift down flat on the surface; this is an unusual tactic, admittedly, but a far less obtrusive way of approaching a swim.

▶ **MELTING IN** Now, even with the light on it, you'll see the float merge in with the debris. Also, if you hold it back slightly, the bait will rise up and the chub will see the bait before any line, shot or anything else disturbs them. Again, it's doing lots of small things right that makes the difference, especially with a difficult fish in clear water.

▶ **FLOAT FREE-LINING** Letting a big bait waft free in the current is a good method for chub. A big lump of flake or a good-sized lobworm is often the bait to use. However, it is easy to lose contact with the bait, as the current manipulates the line into surprising contortions that you'd never guess at from above the water-line. Putting a small float some seven or eight feet up the line can pay dividends. Put the shot to cock the float directly underneath it so that the rest of the line is unencumbered and the bait can rise and fall in the natural fashion that free-lining allows.

Chub and Leger

Most anglers leger for chub because it's easier and, of course, it has done the job for years. However, never underestimate your chub. Richard Walker once said that they take about ten minutes to become unscared for every pound they possess in weight. I'm not so sure about this: I would say a four-pound chub doesn't become unscared after forty minutes, but often as not vacates the area entirely!

If you're legering, never use a lead heavier than you need to – the splash is more easily heard and more harmful. Feather your cast so that the lead lands as lightly as possible on the water; this really helps. It is traditional to quiver tip with the rod pointing to the clouds, but this is problematic here as it makes the line cut through the water at a steep angle, and in sunlight, the rays catch the line and highlight it sharply. Touch legering means the rod tip is down at water level, the line is closer to the river-bed in shallow water and is less likely to be marked out by the sunlight.

◀ **EVER AWARE** This chub, understandably, didn't like the look of me and, typically, is ever aware. Make sure every cast counts, as every time you recast, all you're doing is unsettling the shoal. Also make sure that you get the lead and your bait exactly where you want it the first time. Then leave it – for an hour if you can… two hours, or whatever, until the fish takes.

◀ **A DAGGER OF LIGHT** Shallow, clear water and bright sunlight paint the line from the lead to the rod tip with a banner that spells danger. Lower the rod tip so that the angle of the line through the water is less steep.

▶ **Giveaways** Once you look at terminal tackle down there on the river-bed, you begin to notice all sorts of things that militate against you. You'd never believe how line seems to attract tiny particles of floating weed, for example – it's like a magnet. And, once the line is hung with pieces of vegetation like this it's an absolute give-away to the chub. If I can see it clearly, then I guarantee the fish can do the same.

▶ **Big Impact Baits** Once upon a time, the very best chub bait was a crayfish. Now, obviously, you can't use these highly-protected creatures, but their legacy remains: present a chub with a bait they simply cannot resist and you may get a smash instant take. Big slugs work; lobworms, like this one, can do the trick. Really use your imagination and try anything that excites the chub's interest and, especially, arouses its predatorial instincts.

Taking Care

If the water is at all quick, it will pick even a medium-sized bait off the bottom to play around in the current in a totally unnatural way. Slow water often makes for easier presentation. The problem is that in a negligible flow the fish have all the time in the world to inspect a bait and reject it.

bait wafting about in the current

small shot anchoring bait

SURFACE FEEDING

Seeing fish from beneath the water-line helps one to appreciate the great difference between grazers and predators. The predators lead much less active lives, feeding vigorously, but only for limited periods. The grazers, on the other hand, feed actively over long periods throughout the daylight hours and, when I've happened to observe them on a few night dives, nocturnally as well. And you'd be amazed at just how agile even the biggest carp, bream or tench can prove – they are real athletes of the underwater world. It's my feeling that every grazer – and by that I mean pretty much all freshwater fish apart from perch, pike and zander – will feed enthusiastically on the surface, providing that they're not suspicious or unduly pressured. What do fish actually see when they look up to the surface? Well, I'm not exactly sure about this one myself, yet. There are all sorts of issues to consider – flotsam and jetsam, weeds, reeds, the action of the wind and, above all in clear water, the play of the light from the sun.

▲ AT HOME IN THE LILY PADS This carp is profiting from the cool, the shade and the abundant food stocks. What's surprising, though, is how hard it is for a fish to focus on floating food in bright light.

Carp in the Lilies

If you watch carp in a patch of waterlilies, either below or above the water-line, you can't fail to see that they feed a great deal. Much of their activity can probably be put down to investigative work, combing the underside of lily pads and the long waving stems for anything they might chance upon. They also appear to enjoy lily pads for the shade they give – certainly as a diver, it is extremely pleasant to take refuge under the pads on a very bright day; the light there is greatly diffused and the glare much diminished. Using a floating bait in the lily beds is obviously a great idea, as the pads really do mask the line. It is a good idea, however, to think about using either a very large bait or a highly scented one so that the carp can sense it sooner. If you're close enough, perhaps you could even throw in tiny pellets of mashed bread around the bait – the falling cloud will certainly help a fish home in on it that much more quickly.

▶ **SEEK AND YOU SHALL FIND** Here you are looking at a carp as it sucks in a piece of floating crust. However, what you can't see is the effort that it took to find the piece in the first place. The carp could obviously smell the bread, as it showed great signs of excitement and quite evidently began to hunt around in the area for the food source; but finding the food was a quite different matter – it took the carp a good four or five minutes.

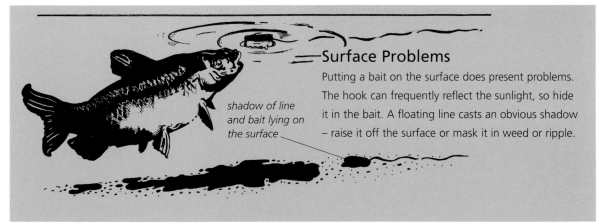

Surface Problems

Putting a bait on the surface does present problems. The hook can frequently reflect the sunlight, so hide it in the bait. A floating line casts an obvious shadow – raise it off the surface or mask it in weed or ripple.

shadow of line and bait lying on the surface

Carp in Sunlight

Having said that carp like the shade of lilies, you do see lots of them in open water, quite evidently enjoying sunlight. Their body language attests loudly to this, whether you watch them from above the surface or below. I'm convinced that when a carp stretches out its fins – the dorsal fin in particular – it's to signal a definite pleasure, and, when the sun is on its back, I suspect it's sheer enjoyment. Oh yes, I'm well aware of the dangers of reading too much into the behaviour of fish, but after spending so many hours alongside them, it is hard not to treat them as sentient creatures.

◀ **TAKING A LOOK** I'm sure that many carp anglers will recognize a lot of what I'm going to say here from their observations above the surface. Quite obviously, we know that carp will investigate a surface bait rigorously. What is not always clear, though, is how many times a certain fish will swim round a particular bait before getting close. I have no doubt that experienced carp test for line on the surface, either with their noses or with their fins. With a large bait, such as a piece of bread crust, they tend to pull it down as an opening gambit once they have a certain amount of faith in it. Often, however, a fish will sit for two minutes or more, wetting the bread further before swallowing, so do not strike prematurely, but wait for a positive movement on the line.

Carp in Open Water

Carp swimming freely in the open spaces of a gravel pit can see line more clearly than when it's hidden by lilies, reeds and the rubbish that accumulates in many marginal bays. Although I'm still unsure whether fish in clear water can see line more or less clearly in piercing sunlight, I am convinced that line is less obvious if it is sunk through the surface film rather than resting on it. Better still, if the situation allows, keep the rod tip up and lift the line off the water's surface. This way, the fish will not be able to feel it either, for, make no mistake, carp will physically search for line as well as looking for it visually. In open water, try to place your bait in a wind channel where the ripple diffuses light and to a degree breaks up the line's profile. Also, play to the carp's inherent greed: feed in particle floaters until desire for food and fear of competition kick in to defeat caution.

▶ **COMPETITION** I've watched carp feed from the surface, cautiously at first, but with increasing abandon as more fish arrive to join in the feast. My advice, therefore, is to resist putting in a hooked bait until a fair amount of activity is taking place. Timing is critical – leave it too late and the keen edge of the fish's hunger is blunted.

▶ **ADDICTED** Certain fish can get hooked on surface feeding. It's my guess that this is particularly the case in waters that aren't food-rich or over-stocked. Certain fish find food more easily in the surface film than on the bed, and this is where a big, meaty bait can work well, especially on a water where smaller cat and dog biscuits, for example, are commonly used.

Chub with Crust and Flake

We all know that chub have keen eyesight, but my own observations suggest that they can see pieces of crust at least five yards upstream of them, especially when the water is clear and with little breeze. Of course, the smell of the bait approaching could also have something to do with this; chub frequently seem to become agitated before the bait actually comes into sight. What you can't see from the bank, however, is that the chub will follow a specific piece of floating bait for several yards, almost certainly watching for it to pull off course or behave in any way unnaturally. There's a problem for the angler here, as if you mend the line this will look very obvious from below. I'd suggest as fine a line as you can get away with allied with a long roach rod to cushion the lunges of the chub through the fight. If you can wade out so that you're in as direct a line as possible to that floating piece of bait, so much the better.

◀ **INSPECTION** As the floating bait comes close, there is a lot of bubbling around it and general nosing. Once again, as in the case of carp, I'm convinced that the chub is looking for any hint of line.

◀ **DECISION** When a chub does make its mind up, it will hold the bait between its lips and drop down a fair way to suck the bait in properly and to chew it. My obvious tip, therefore, is to wait for the line to tighten and go away before striking. If you strike as soon as you see the bread disappear, you will miss virtually every fish.

SUMMER STILLWATERS

There's an almost sacred beauty about a picturesque stillwater seen in the shafts of summer sunlight. Its beauty is reflected in some of the more forgotten species today, such as the rudd and the crucian, and confirmed by the majesty of carp and tench. All lake species demonstrate an endless array of fascinating habits. Once again, these are mirrored in the dynamics of the water they inhabit. From the surface, the summer pool may well look calm and unruffled but, beneath, it is all vitality and explosive change. For example, weeds can grow inches, if not feet, in a single day. Insect hatches can be pulsating – especially when the midges are rising into the soft, evening air. At times like this everything becomes energized, with frantically feeding fish snapping at the emerging insects and, as often as not, perch and pike harrying them in turn.

▲ FISHING A SHADED POOL As the light begins to set, look for areas of water where the debris of the day lies thickly in the surface. Fish are attracted to the amount of dead and dying insect life here.

Rudd and Lilies

If there are lilies on a water, then rudd will almost inevitably be among them, smaller ones especially. The reasons aren't that difficult to find: food, shade, protection from predators... they're even quite adept at skipping out of the water and lying for a few seconds on the top of a pad should a pike attack from beneath!

From looking at the many shots of rudd shoals that I've taken, it seems as if there are always one or two fish searching the water away from the direction in which the main body of rudd are moving. It's as though they are scanning 360°, presumably for pike or perch attack. This behavioural pattern is less marked when the shoal is moving fast, but then, generally, it has sensed trouble and is making its escape. You will often find rudd attacking a single food source if it's prevalent enough but, under most conditions, they will hang at all manner of depths sipping in food of every type – nymphs, water shrimps, bloodworm, buzzers.

◀ PROTECTIVE BEHAVIOUR There are a couple of interesting points here. As mentioned above, there is one of the shoal apparently keeping guard from a possible attack from the rear. Also, note the gleam of light on the leading fish as they move between the pads. It's my belief that right now they are most vulnerable to a pike attack. It's as though the flash awakens even a dormant fish.

◀ THE LILY JUNGLE A mass of lilies such as this one looks impressive from the top, but wait until you actually get in among them. There, you'll find an endless variation in light patterns and even quite noticeable temperature changes. The roots of a well-established lily bed are also massively tangled, ancient and all but impossible to uproot.

▶ **LAYERED FEEDING** Rudd are especially adept at feeding from the upper layers of water, and this makes them the perfect target for the fly angler. However, they are equally alert to food in mid-water and on the bottom… slow sinking flake and maggots are, therefore, perfect baits. Don't expect to hold a rudd shoal for long, whatever bait you present them with – their fear of predators keeps them constantly on the alert, always ready to move along.

▼ **ON THE PROWL** I do like this shot of a pike taken on a summer's day in a lily bed. It really is the perfect, mean, little predator, weighing in at five or six pounds, I guess. The rudd in the vicinity will recognize all the signs of aggression. Note how the fish is poised at 45° or so, its ideal attack angle. What the stills camera can't get across is the quiet menace of the pike, with its fins rippling and its eyes swivelling, focusing intently on any signs of life or potential food swimming above it.

Food in the Lilies

Rudd are great grazers, especially when they weigh under a pound, and they will feed for most of the daylight hours. This makes them particularly catchable and great sport for youngsters. A pair of binoculars is a good idea for picking out where the rudd shoals are roaming – you may well see either the flash of their scales or the exquisite red banner fins. Very frequently, you will just see the lily pads quiver as the fish rub against the stems.

Although crucian carp are primarily bottom feeders, they may also feed near the surface. What they do always require though, is cover. For that reason, lily beds are the ideal crucian haunt. Within them, crucians can feel confident enough to feed near the surface.

◀ **Fishing in Tight** You can't beat float fishing in amongst the pads, but make sure that the float gets right in there. I like the way a bait drops naturally through the water without any weight attached. Bunch the shot under the float so it cocks immediately and lets the bait waiver down in as natural a fashion as possible. Maggots and other light baits on a hook frequently fall unnaturally. Think of something a little bit heavier – a red worm is ideal.

◀ **An Invitation to Feed** This two-pound crucian is photographed slurping in breadflake from the surface itself, attracted out from its refuge among the lily pads. It's a good idea to get a real rubby-dubby of bread mash going in the lily beds – you'll attract rudd, tench, crucians and even a passing mirror or common carp.

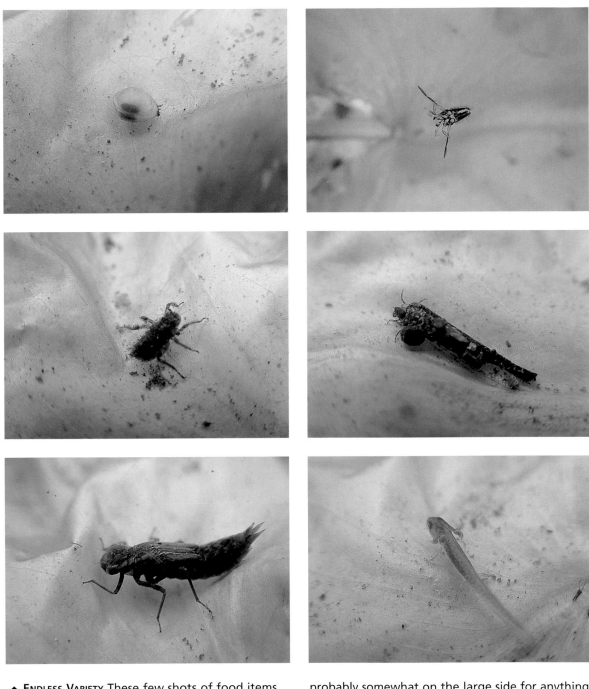

▲ ENDLESS VARIETY These few shots of food items in the lily bed just go a fraction of the way towards showing the variety that is on offer. Water shrimps, water fleas, pea mussels, water boatmen, emerging insects, beetles and fry all find their way into the gullets of rudd. Caddis (centre right) are one of the most common food items, whilst the dragonfly nymph (bottom left) is probably somewhat on the large side for anything other than a bigger fish. By the way, carp are also incredibly aggressive creatures and will investigate anything moving in their territory... I've even seen one attack a great ramshorn snail! One unexpected food source is a baby newt (bottom right), which stands little chance of survival in waters thickly inhabited by carp.

Big Rudd

Big rudd, in my diving experiences, appear to behave rather differently to their smaller brethren. The change in behaviour seems to take place when they reach a weight of between a pound and a pound and a half, probably when they feel less vulnerable to pike attacks. In short, they are more willing to leave cover and investigate what their whole environment can offer them.

Big rudd appear to be very mobile, and it's a good idea to put out a stream of baits if you're fishing with a floater on the surface. If you're trying to catch them from the lake-bed, however, don't expect to hold a shoal of big rudd for long. Get a bed of particles down, as this gives you the best chance of maintaining their interest for as long as possible. Try putting par-boiled, white-grained rice into your feeder mix – they love it, and the tiny grains keep them hunting for long periods.

◀ **CRUISING** There is a large amount of insect life drifting on, or just beneath, the surface of any stillwater, and big rudd go with the currents, exploiting this food source. At night, their distinctive, splashing way of breaking surface is due partly to their technique of pulling down moths from the air itself. A large dry fly – a mayfly pattern – can be just as successful as a caster or a dog biscuit.

◀ **ON THE BOTTOM** Don't believe the old textbooks that say the protruding bottom lip of the rudd makes it difficult for them to feed on the lake bed. Nonsense! Big rudd are just as happy to graze bloodworm beds, for example, as any tench or carp. And that's very good news for the angler who wants to fish for them on the bottom at night with traditional swim feeder techniques.

Tench Feeding

Observations above and below the water-line lead me to suggest that tench have well-defined patrol routes, and you will find the same fish in the same areas at the same times, day after day. They move in loose shoals, often predominantly male or female. As we know, tench feed early in the day, but feeding spells frequently last longer than we think. As the light grows, they can simply see us, our tackle and any defects in our presentation more clearly, and they will make fewer mistakes. They are especially adept at picking up line falling from a float through mid-water; after sunrise a lead or a feeder with a small back lead can work more efficiently.

▲ **DAWN PATROL** This shot was taken around five o'clock one June morning. Masses of bubbles indicated plenty of feeding tench, but bites were few. Either the fish were preoccupied with a natural food source, such as bloodworms, or they were suspicious of the terminal gear. One solution is to change to a lighter hook or a neutral-density bait, such as flake, or a floating caster/maggot combination.

▶ **JUST RESTING** Look carefully and you'll see the tench, a couple of pounds in weight, well hidden and seemingly in the land of nod. It certainly isn't objecting to my presence.

◀ **A WARY EYE** However, as I present this piece of breadflake very close to the tench and swim back a yard or so, he begins to show evident interest. His eye swivels until he makes contact with the bait. His fins begin to work, and you can sense that he is weighing up a thorough investigation. Eventually, sadly, he moves slowly backwards and disappears totally into the weed growth.

▼ **STAYING TOGETHER** This illustrates how tench like to behave in full light in smaller waters. You can see them searching the shade afforded by old, wooden sheathing, designed to keep the bank intact. Tench, rather like barbel, also like the comfort of friends and the feeling of fin against fin, body against body when they are in this semi-sleep mode. However, they can be enticed to take a big-impact bait, such as a lively lobworm, if it is positioned very close.

▲ **A FEEDING TENCH** When they are feeding, tench swim slowly a little way above the bottom looking intently downwards for signs of food activity. In this mode, they will also suck in free-swimming insects. When it decides on a patch to investigate, it will move down head first and feed at virtually 90°. This habit gives quite a number of line bites when float fishing. This, I believe, is why laying-on has been so successful over the years; it simply means that a tench over the bait is well away from any line dropping down from the float.

▶ **BREAM HABITS** Big bream can be very old and hugely experienced. They have good eyesight, and those big deep bodies of theirs give them plenty of chance to feel line in mid-water. For those reasons, I prefer legering with the line pinned out of the way on the bottom. Like tench, bream are reluctant to pick up a heavy or unnatural looking bait between their lips, preferring to suck in smaller, lighter items.

Big Tench

The behaviour of big tench differs, in my experience, from that of smaller fish; they have larger territories and they frequently inhabit much bigger waters. Certainly, the new, large and comparatively barren pits seem to suit them very well. Food is plentiful in this environment and competition is frequently minimal.

What to catch them with? Hook baits? Well, lobworms are a bit of a quandary for me – I've seen big tench catch sight of them, quiver with anticipation and move rapidly well over a yard to pick them up. Equally, I've watched a fish shy away from a lob when it's been virtually under its nose. When bites have been impossible to come by, I'd advise giving a lobworm a whirl if you're fairly sure that there are feeding tench in the area – it's always worth a try.

◀ **MOVING INTO THE LIGHT** Big tench in large open waters seem to be remarkably unafraid of the light compared with smaller fish in heavily weeded ones. Admittedly, they do like the shade of lilies or bulrushes, but they are happy to feed out in bright, open sunlight, as you can see from this photograph.

◀ **PATROLLING** From what I've seen, one of the biggest problems catching fish in this type of water is actual location. The tench will often seem to patrol quite large areas – certainly several hundred yards is not uncommon. It is often important to lay down a carpet of bait and wait for the fish to come onto it. If you can prebait for several days, there is all the more chance of focusing the fish tightly.

Observations

It's obvious that the more time you spend looking at a water and getting to know it, either from above or below the water-line, the more you'll begin to understand. Equally, however, the more it can prove to be a puzzle! I offer you these three shots, along with some possible solutions. It is important for any angler to patrol the bankside, preferably with binoculars, and look for feeding fish before deciding on a pitch and putting out bait into an area that may be barren of fish.

▸ **FEEDING FRENZY** Wow! What you're seeing here is almost the entire carp population of a twenty-acre lake gathered in one north-west corner. They are feeding frantically, stirring the water to a soup. I've witnessed this behaviour on half a dozen occasions over the last ten years or so, but I'm still not exactly sure of the cause. Perhaps a particularly rich bloodworm bed has been discovered and the feeding activity has drawn in group after group of carp.

▸ **GRUB UP?** Now, I would never advise using a live newt as carp bait. However, I have to say that my own observations lead me to believe that a carp, especially a decent-sized one, is very, very partial to a passing newt. Are there any particularly bold carp anglers out there willing to experiment with one of the modern, excellent plastic imitations now on the market? Jigging fools ultra-sharp fish such as black bass, so it could be well worth a try.

▲ **PULLED BY THE CLOUD** Now, what's going on here, you might ask? But there's a simple explanation. I was, in fact, lying in a pool in Morocco watching some quite large fish in thick reed beds. I'm not, to this day, absolutely certain what they were, but they were definitely members of the carp family. The fish were extremely reluctant to approach me. However, every time I reached out a hand to disturb the silt in front of them, they would come out to investigate – every single time. It made me remember just how successful a technique dragging for tench used to be back in the 1950s and '60s, and how it's been overlooked in the modern age. Perhaps dragging could become a rediscovered art form for tench, carp and, definitely, perch.

raking up the bottom releases all kinds of food items

The Art of Dragging

A rake pronged on both sides, a decent length of rope, and you are in business. Simply throw it out, let it sink and drag it back through the silt. Scents and a host of tiny foodstuffs are released, drawing in tench, perch and bream. You are also clearing the swim of heavy weed growth and helping your presentation. Just check with other anglers around the lake first!

SUMMER SMALL FRY

In truth, the fish I have in mind may be small, but they are utterly engaging. Take a tip – spend an afternoon out on the water. Choose warm weather and bright sunlight and wade, turning over rocks. Look for crayfish, loach, bullheads and even small river lampreys. Build up a picture of the river from the viewpoint of the mini species. Look under the stones and you'll be amazed at the aquatic life there. And what about the bigger fish – dace are as lovely and fascinating as other fish ten times their size and, for sheer subtlety of colour, you can't beat the gudgeon with its dusky blue fins and oatmeal-coloured fins. Sometimes you will be able to lower yourself under the water-line of a summer millpond, especially when sluices are closed down. You will enter a world of frenetic activity – there are fish everywhere, from half an inch to ten, fifteen

or twenty inches in length. Sometimes, if you cast in a feeder, you will attract a great, black dome of tiny fish pecking at the food cloud as it descends to the bottom. Oh, to be a two-pound perch – the living just couldn't be easier! You'd be surprised, though, at the number of species that do prey on the small fry… chub, barbel, bream and eels are all happy to take fingerlings.

◀ SUMMER FISHING A millpond at the height of summer is a great place to witness the organic wealth of a river system.

Maggot Strategies

Take light gear and a pint of maggots to the summer river and you'll be amazed at the variety of fish on offer. In all probability, you won't catch anything very large, but that's really not the issue – it's the variety that counts. Looked at from underneath the water, it's quite apparent why the match man's approach and tackle is the effective way to catch under these conditions.

◀ **LOOSE FEED** Loose-fed maggots energize a wide area. They also build up activity from the surface of the water right down to the bottom as several species of varying sizes attack the maggots at the different levels. Minnows tend to pick at the surface; such fish as dace can be found in mid-water; while gudgeon, small roach and perch grub over the bottom remains. All this activity can also cause larger predatorial fish to move in – and that includes barbel and chub, as well as pike and larger perch.

◀ **THE FEEDER** A swim feeder, quite obviously, operates differently: the feeding area that is built up is more restricted, and bottom-feeding fish tend to be targeted. Moreover, it's much easier to present a couple of hooked maggots on a feeder rig than it is to trot a single maggot convincingly along with free-falling offerings.

◀ **SELF-HOOKED** This gudgeon mopped up five or six maggots before it came upon the hook bait. It simply sucked the bait in and then turned to go. In this shot, its head is pulling against the weight of the feeder and there you have it, a hooked gudgeon. Really, the bolt-rig is a long-established method, and not nearly as complex as some would have us believe.

The Float

There's really only one way to catch dace and that's by float fishing. Dace will take bait on the bottom, of course, but that's to deny the whole essence of what fishing for them is about. It's light, it's tight, it's delicate and it's great fun. However, the float does present problems all of its own – only strike when you are quite sure you have a bite, and try to keep that strike as controlled as you can. Remember the age-old adage that the merest flick of the wrist suffices.

▶ **RIDING NICELY** A little stick float, accurately shotted, breasts the current, taking its offering of maggots down a swim some three or four feet deep where dace are numerous. Loose-fed maggots build the swim up nicely and everything looks set for good sport.

▶ **HELD BACK** No matter what you're fishing for, holding back the bait is a great idea. In part, this is the induced take: a fish can't resist the sight of a bait lifting tantalizingly in front of its nose. The other advantage is that the fish sees the bait first rather than the shot, the line or the float itself. This is an important point, especially in clear water with fish that are in the least bit educated.

▶ **A STRIKE** The float has been held back, the bait's been taken and a strike has just been made. This mini-explosion of surface water is what you see from just beneath the water-line. It doesn't matter how deep or shallow, how slow or fast the river is or how bright the day, this explosion will occur to some degree or other. Obviously, on a bright day on a shallow swim, this starburst does nothing to encourage fish to feed confidently.

Dace and Bullheads

The beauty and the beast of the summer river... no wonder dace are often called the dart. Under water all you sometimes see of them is a little blur of silver. As for the bullhead, well no wonder it's often called the miller's thumb. Short, squat and head-heavy, with a mouth that opens from ear to ear. However, under the water, you realize that both have their place in this fragile, fascinating environment.

▲ **THE DART** Here they are, constantly on the move, flitting like tiny silver arrows through the shallow, sun-dappled summer river. You don't always have to learn something new when you go under water – sometimes it's just enough to sit there on the river-bed watching and marvelling at how beautiful and complex the underwater cycle of life can be.

◀ **THE BOTTOM HUGGER** This is just about as much of a bullhead as you're likely to see during the daylight hours, as they spend the bulk, if not all, of their time under the nearest algae-covered stone. But it all changes after dark – then you'll see the bullheads having a ball. In places, the bed can seem absolutely paved with these fish. Suddenly, they become energetic, even frolicsome, as they dig for food and suck in insects from the drift of water above them.

FISHING A WINTER RIVER

Underwater observations suggest to me that fish move around much more slowly in the winter river than the summer one. I suppose you'd expect that, as temperatures plummet and the whole life-cycle slows down. However, there is movement. Shoals of roach, especially, can be quite lively, particularly when there's a tinge of colour in the water – something you'd expect from your catch records. But this doesn't mean that location is not central to success on any winter session. Roach definitely hang close to cover. Look for dead cabbage beds, for example, sunken trees or anything that breaks up their outline and gives them a feeling of protection. Depth is also an issue. I generally find them in water over five feet deep, but there are exceptions. In the river

featured in this photograph, for example, they move into water just two or three feet deep upstream of the mill. Don't make the mistake of going for the deadest water you can find – often you will find roach shoals deliberately seeking out water with some push to it. So my perfect winter roach swim? I'd look for water around six to eight feet deep but perhaps shelving up towards the end of the run. There will be some flow and definitely a number of snags.

◄ **BRIGHT DAYS** Roach are always unpredictable. Although they favour warm westerly winds and a coloured river, bright sunlight can spark them into unexpected movement.

The River and its Roach

A big roach in winter is one of the craftiest creatures alive. If the water is clear and cold, then the roach's inherent wariness is magnified. You, therefore, must think very carefully about your bait and how best to present it. Light feeding – sprinkling in tiny amounts of bait until, one by one, fish begin to feed and eventually a whole spree is triggered – is often a good idea. Also, bites can be very gentle indeed, and your indication must be precise.

Unless a river is heavily in flood, float fishing is a great form of attack, as it does search out greater amounts of water than the leger ever can. One tip though: try to retrieve your float close to the bank rather than through the swim itself, as winter roach are neurotically afraid of disturbance over their heads.

◀ **AMIDST THE CLUTTER** Mid-winter, a swim around five feet deep and a shoal of roach is moving through comparatively gloomy water. It's a good roach swim – there's plenty of clutter around to break up their movement, and lots of food hidden in the bottom vegetation. Mind you, trotting a swim as dirty as this down on the bottom is pretty well impossible. Go for a light leger instead.

◀ **OVERKILL** Put in too much loose feed and you will kill a swim like this stone dead. I've seen it happen – I've put in too much mash, too many casters or too many maggots and found them on the bottom days later, ignored and beginning to rot.

▶ **Making a Move** At last a roach moves towards a falling caster. It gets to within a couple of inches or so, flares its gills, creates a vacuum and whips in that grub faster than the eye can see. One moment it's there – and a fraction of a second later, it's gone.

▶ **A Lesson for the Angler** The caster is in the mouth and soon the roach begins to chew. A sight like this makes you realize why match anglers catch so many fish in the winter, whereas bigger bait men, like me, struggle. An intricate shotting pattern helps to present a small bait like this with maximum delicacy, whereas a heavy shot close to the hook would never allow that unrestricted suck in.

▶ **Flood Problems** The enrichment of so many of our lowland rivers by agricultural run-off has led to huge increases in silkweed and algae. Once winter comes along, this begins to die off and it trundles downriver in seemingly endless quantities throughout the dark months, clogging the line and pulling bait out of position. Sometimes, it seems, there is no way to combat it. Try fishing as close in as possible and in stretches where there is less rubbish in the flow.

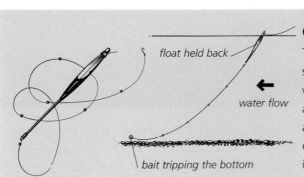

float held back

water flow

bait tripping the bottom

Careful Trotting

Trotting a bait like this is tremendously effective for several major reasons. Firstly, and obviously, a lot of water is covered. Secondly, bites, even delicate ones, are instantly seen. Thirdly, the bait is introduced with a minimum of splash. Lastly, and vitally, the shot down the line is held back from the fish and the bait is the first thing that they see.

Roach Perils

Believe me, the life of a roach is not an easy one. Cormorants, pike, floods, disease, pollution and anglers – these are just a few of the threats to the roach's safety. The school of hard knocks has made a big river roach a very wary creature indeed. Public enemy number one is almost undoubtedly the pike, even though a roach knows full well how to interpret its body language. I'm not sure quite what triggers a pike into feeding mode, but I have a feeling that bright sunlight plays a part. I'm not saying that bright water conditions are necessarily best for pike fishing, but it is the light that kick-starts resting fish back into life. If you manage to get a catch, remember that keeping fish in nets is not a good idea. In matches, I accept they are necessary, but outside of matches we must phase them out if we really care about the good of our fish stocks.

▲ THE MENACE For most of the winter, pike lie doggo on the bottom of a river-bed. Often the river will have piled silt and scraps of dead weed over them as they lie virtually unmoving for days on end. At times like this, you will find roach lying within inches of the seemingly moribund predator, but as soon as the pike's fins begin to move and the eyes begin to roll, it's a different matter altogether…

▶ **DEATH SENTENCE** This keep net that I came across was small, quite old-fashioned and staked out by a couple of lads who were ignorant of this miserable scene below the water-line. Modern keep nets are more fish-friendly physically, but the psychological stress is still there and should be avoided.

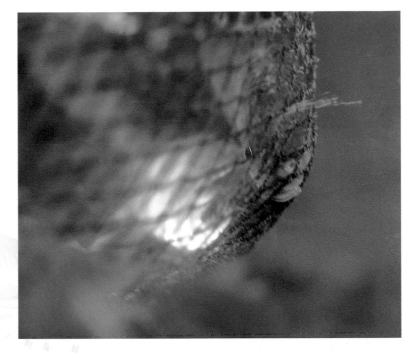

▲ **A PEARL OF NATURE** This is how a roach should look – glistening silver, fins absolutely perfect and lips totally undamaged or torn. As the late, great Hugh Falkus said, 'It's a beauty such as this that makes getting up on a freezing dawn morning or staying on well after the sun has set and the frost is beginning to form worthwhile'. Falkus, a master of sea-trout rivers, was wise enough to appreciate the beauty of the apparently humble roach.

CATCHING AND CARING FOR MAHSEER

Now I've leapt from roach to mahseer – the greatest sporting fish of India. I like this juxtaposition of the giant and the dwarf, if only to emphasize that they both have their place in the great scheme of things and both are fascinating when viewed up close. But, I have to admit, mahseer are particularly so! In fact, they offer the greatest challenge of any freshwater fish I've personally come up against. First of all, mahseer fight ferociously – that is, if you can hook one to begin with. There is true savagery in the way they thrash that rod down, desperate to wrench it from your grasp. In this they're aided by a supremely powerfully built body and fins the size of tennis racquets. And, of course, by the rivers they inhabit. Indian rivers tend to be huge, muscular as pythons and invariably studded with rocks. The mahseer, in layman's terms, is half-carp, half-barbel, with the accumulated wisdom of both. They live long, they appear to remember what they see and they know their river intimately. The resulting animal is a beast that is notoriously hard to catch and downright brutal if you succeed.

▲ **AN INDIAN ADVENTURE** The Indian dawn and, heart in mouth, the intrepid angler sets off in the coracle with his ghillie. What will the day's sport bring him?

Bait in a Pool

Diving in India is a delight, with its warm rivers and crystal clarity. Providing, of course, you don't mind the snakes and other river creepy crawlies! Fishing big pools – some are half a mile long and up to two hundred yards wide – can be an unnerving experience. You know there are big fish present – you can often feel them against the line, even picking up the bait between their huge lips – but these great Indian fish can be as cautious as any you will come up against.

The water in the pools can be almost wholly slack and this can provide advantages. Your bait presentation can be made more perfect, and I like the way the lead almost invariably begins to sink into the bottom mud – this occurs after a minute or so – while the bait sits unobtrusively on the river-bed. In many pools, after perhaps ten to fifteen minutes, the lead is completely hidden, which is a real bonus, believe me. The problem is that the slower the water, the more time any mahseer has to inspect the bait and the terminal rig. In fact, it can take all the time in the world – and it frequently does!

▶ **An Indian Lead** Indians make these long spiral weights out of sheets of building lead. Here, you can see a weight, weighing two or three ounces, lying in the soft mud of a big pool.

▶ **Ragi Paste** These great balls of millet and other secret substances are the original, mind-blowing boily. Often weighing three or four ounces, they can be as large as a small orange. In a still pool, you can present them in the most natural-looking fashion. They simply rest there and become almost as one with the surrounding mud and silt. It's sometimes a good idea to put little pieces of lead between the main spiral and the ragi itself so that the line sinks further into the silt. In this way, your presentation can become almost perfect.

Bait in Rapids

I couldn't begin to say whether mahseer prefer to feed in the pools or the rapids. The fact is, they will go to different water types to find different foods. In the rapids, the mahseer are looking for small fish and crab, and they certainly love feeding in rocky crevices for any titbits they can find. However, here the food has a habit of disappearing quickly and the mahseer can't delay too long over a decision. Sometimes the mahseer makes the wrong decision and this is when the angler has the advantage.

◀ **ON ROCK** The problem here is plain to see. The lead goes nowhere in the comparatively shallow, clear, quick water under a blazing Indian sun. It sits proud and reflects back the sun almost hypnotically. Make no mistake, the mahseer can see a problem like this from several yards away.

◀ **THE APPROACH** A big mahseer comes close to a piece of ragi. The water is really pushing over this rock, gushing through the fish's gills and over its scales.

◀ **THE STRINGER** The hooked mahseer is traditionally tied to a stringer and follows the coracle downstream, supposedly building up strength for its release. I think the stringer does have its place, but be careful how you use it. String a fish for half an hour or so, but perhaps don't move it from the pool in which it was landed. Once its strength returns, slip the knot and let it glide back to the cool depths.

Mahseer Care

Conservation is vital, not only for the fish – and in this I don't just mean mahseer, but all breeds of fish – but also for the future of fishing in general. One thing that diving has taught me is that fish are fragile, stunningly beautiful and masters of their own environment. We must respect these qualities – the Indians certainly do. They have always regarded mahseer as the king of fish and deserving of the best possible care. You'll rarely see any photograph of a mahseer that doesn't have glistening scales and droplets of water on its fins because all the guides insist on this. Dunk the fish, hold it in the air for a few seconds... click, click,... and back it goes.

▶ **KING OF FISH** My great friend and guide, Dassy, with my own best black mahseer of thirty pounds. These are among the most rare of mahseer sub-species, but only recently I witnessed the capture of a seventy-pounder – a magnificent creature.

▶ **A TEAM EFFORT** In India, the guides are central to the capture of every mahseer. Without them, we'd never succeed at all. But that's what fishing is all about – learning, appreciating and sharing marvellous experiences with firm and trusted friends.

Author's Acknowledgements

My greatest thanks for encouragement, inspiration, generosity and friendship go to Johnny Jensen and Martin Hayward Smith; both are expert photographers who have collaborated with me so closely on these works – I cannot possibly overstate their contribution.

Thank you also to Kevin Cullimore for showing me the way, back in the 1990s. Thank you to the late and dearly missed Mike Smith at Bure Valley Fisheries, Mike Taylor at the Red Lion in Bredwardine, Bill Makins at Pensthorpe and Paul Seaman for all your help with locations.

Thank you in Spain to Peter, Rafa and Ignatio… marvellous men and anglers all.

Thank you to all the following for your help either in fishing situations or for your copious and wise advice: Alan Felstead, Leo Grosze Nipper, Sue and Chris Harris, Reuben Hook, Phil Humm, Simon MacMillan, Robert Malone, Rob Olsen, Christopher West and Jo Whorisky.

Thank you to Steve at Ocean Optronics, and to Fergus Granville in North Uist.

Thank you to all at Design Revolution, and special thanks to Carol, who has had to contend with a mass of woolly-minded thoughts from yours truly.